THIS PRODUCT IS INTENDED FOR HOME USE ONLY

The images and all other content in this book are copyrighted material owned by Elemental Science, Inc. Please do not reproduce this content on email lists or websites. If you have an eBook, you may print out as many copies as you need for use WITHIN YOUR IMMEDIATE FAMILY ONLY. Duplicating this book or printing the eBook so that the book can then be reused or resold is a violation of copyright.

Schools and co-ops: You MAY NOT DUPLICATE OR PRINT any portion of this book for use in the classroom. Please contact us for licensing options at support@elementalscience.com.

Summer's Lab - Student Lab Manual

First Edition, Second Printing 2022
Copyright @ Elemental Science, Inc.

ISBN: 978-1-935614-72-2

For more copies write to:

Elemental Science
PO Box 79
Niceville, FL 32588
Email: support@elementalscience.com

Copyright Policy

All contents copyright © 2020, 2022 by Elemental Science. All rights reserved.

LIMIT OF LIABILITY AND DISCLAIMER OF WARRANTY: The publisher has used its best efforts in preparing this book, and the information provided herein is provided "as is." Elemental Science makes no representation or warranties with respect to the accuracy or completeness of the contents of this book and specifically disclaims any implied warranties of merchantability or fitness for any particular purpose and shall in no event be liable for any loss of profit or any other commercial damage, including but not limited to special, incidental, consequential, or other damages.

TRADEMARKS: This book identifies product names and services known to be trademarks, registered trademarks, or service marks of their respective holders. They are used throughout this book in an editorial fashion only. In addition, terms suspected of being trademarks, registered trademarks, or service marks have been appropriately capitalized, although Elemental Science cannot attest to the accuracy of this information. Use of a term in this book should not be regarded as affecting the validity of any trademark, registered trademark, or service mark. Elemental Science is not associated with any product or vendor mentioned in this book.

LAB MANUAL TABLE OF CONTENTS

A Welcome from Summer Beach 5

Unit 1: Animals 7

    Amphibians   8

    Birds   12

    Reptiles   16

    Insects   20

Unit 2: Humans 25

    Living Things   26

    Mammals   30

    Body Cells   34

    Human Body   38

Unit 3: Plants 43

    Plants   44

    Flowers   48

    Seeds   52

    Trees   56

Unit 4: Weather 61

    The Sun   62

    Clouds   66

    Weather   70

    Seasons   74

Unit 5: Rocks 79

    Rocks   80

    Mountains   84

Volcanoes	88	
Fossils	92	

Unit 6: Space 97

The Moon	98
Astronauts	102
Our Solar System	106
Stars	110

Unit 7: Matter 115

Atoms	116
Liquids and Solids	120
Freezing and Melting	124
Mixtures and Solutions	128

Unit 8: Energy 133

Forces	134
Sound	138
Light	142
Magnets	146

INTRODUCTION
A Welcome from Summer Beach

Welcome to Summer's Lab!! I am Summer Beach, research scientist, Sassy-Sci supporter, and your host for this journey!

You may have heard about me through *The Sassafras Science Adventures* series, but if you haven't that is totally fine! I have known Cecil Sassafras, inventor of the invisible zip lines, for years, and I had a blast helping him teach his nephew, Blaine, and niece, Tracey, all about science. So when the twins (Blaine and Tracey) asked me to create an introduction to science, well . . . I have to admit I was floored!

Ulysses had to wave a toasted roast beef, cheddar cheese, tomato, and horseradish sandwich, which happens to be my favorite kind, under my nose just to get me to respond! I quickly recovered and Ulysses and I set to work. In case you don't know, Ulysses is my lab assistant, who also happens to be an arctic ground squirrel. He's quite the helpful mammal, although he does disappear each winter for hibernation, which can be a bit tricky if we are mid-project!

So now that you know a bit about me, let me tell you about your upcoming adventure. Ulysses and I are opening the doors to our lab to give you a hands-on journey through science for the very first time. Each week we will be building a science sandwich that you will want to gobble up!

We will be learning about animals, plants, weather, rocks, matter, and forces. And you will work on your observations skills as you help us out in the lab.

Ulysses and I hope that you enjoy this year of sandwich science from our lab!

STUDENT LAB MANUAL AT-A-GLANCE

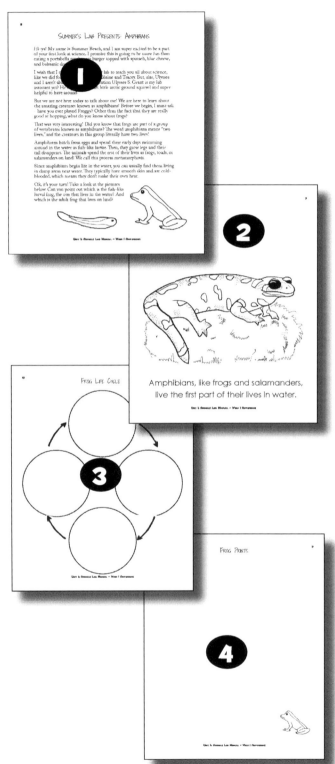

Create a beautiful memory of your science-filled sandwich-loving journey!

THE LAB MANUAL

Think of the *Summer's Lab Student Lab Manual* as your scrapbook-style workbook. It's your place to write down or draw what you have learned in Summer's Lab. Here is what you will see each week:

1. Science Stories

Each of these stories will introduce the science topic you are learning for the week with and sandwich and a smile!

2. Coloring Pages

As your teacher reads the week's science story to you, you can color these pages. Then, you can read (or memorize) the sentence on it to help you remember the most important fact from the week.

3. Hands-on Project Sheets

These sheets provide space for you to write down what you did for the hands-on project.

4. Activity Sheets

These sheets allow you to do the week's main activity.

SEE IT ALL AT:
https://elementalscience.com/collections/summers-lab

SUMMER'S LAB

Unit 1: Animals

Student Lab Manual

Summer's Lab Presents: Amphibians

Hi-ya! My name is Summer Beach, and I am super excited to be a part of your first look at science. I promise this is going to be more fun than eating a portabella mushroom burger topped with spinach, blue cheese, and balsamic dressing!

I wish that I could zip you all to my lab to teach you all about science, like we did for the Sassafras twins, Blaine and Tracey. But, alas, Ulysses and I aren't able to do so. Did I mention Ulysses S. Grant is my lab assistant yet? He's quite the smart little arctic ground squirrel and super helpful to have around.

But we are not here today to talk about me! We are here to learn about the amazing creatures known as amphibians! Before we begin, I must ask - have you ever played Froggy? Other than the fact that they are really good at hopping, what do you know about frogs?

That was very interesting! Did you know that frogs are part of a group of vertebrates known as amphibians? The word amphibians means "two lives," and the creatures in this group literally have two lives!

Amphibians hatch from eggs and spend their early days swimming around in the water as fish-like larvae. Then, they grow legs and their tail disappears. The animals spend the rest of their lives as frogs, toads, or salamanders on land! We call this process metamorphosis.

Since amphibians begin life in the water, you can usually find them living in damp areas near water. They typically have smooth skin and are cold-blooded, which means they don't make their own heat.

OK, it's your turn! Take a look at the pictures below. Can you point out which is the fish-like larval frog, the one that lives in the water? And which is the adult frog that lives on land?

Unit 1: Animals Lab Manual - Week 1 Amphibians

Amphibians, like frogs and salamanders, live the first part of their lives in water.

Frog Life Cycle

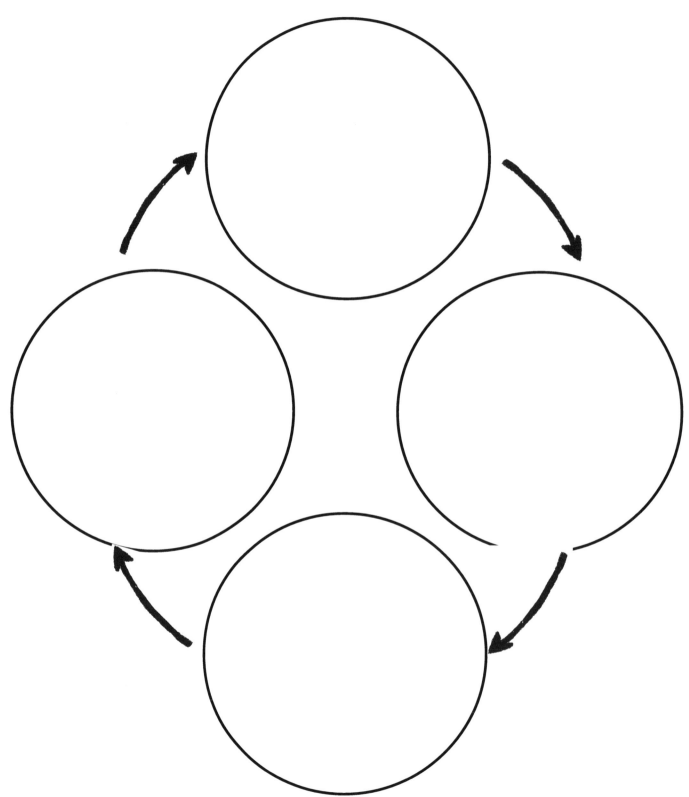

Frog Prints

Unit 1: Animals Lab Manual - Week 1 Amphibians

Summer's Lab Presents: Birds

Ulysses and I were recently on our first spring picnic, scarfing down our sandwiches – bagels with smoked salmon and capers, yumm-o – when we spotted some ptarmigan. The birds were moving in and out of the rocks, quietly searching for a meal of early spring willow buds.

I love to spot birds in Alaska in the spring because they are molting, which means they are losing their extra winter feathers. Ulysses and I like to gather these up to use for different projects and experiments in the lab!

Before I share with you a bit more about birds, why don't you tell me more about what you know about these animals?

You are so smart!! Birds do have feathers covering their bodies, instead of the fur or hair that mammals have. The feathers help to keep them warm and help the bird to be able to fly. Birds also have wings instead of arms, which really gives them the advantage when it comes to flying.

Birds lay eggs and then sit on them for several weeks to keep them warm. Inside the egg, a baby bird develops, and when it is ready, it uses a special beak called an "egg-tooth" to break out! Mama bird feeds the baby partially digested food, a.k.a. puke, until it is big enough to fly out of the nest and find its own food. So glad that I am a mammal and my mom fed me milk instead!!

OK, it is your turn! Can you find the wings and feathers on the eagle?

Birds have wings and feathers.

Cheerio Bird Feeder

This is who visited the bird feeder:

_____

_____

_____

_____

_____

_____

Unit 1: Animals Lab Manual - Week 2 Birds

Painting with Feathers

Summer's Lab Presents: Reptiles

A couple of years back, Ulysses and I were in Arizona checking out the Grand Canyon and the Petrified National Forest – which, by the way, totally rock! – when we had our very first smoked rattlesnake sandwich. I must confess that I am a bit afraid of snakes, so the thought of eating one didn't really rank high on my "Sandwiches-to-try" list. But I have to admit, it wasn't half bad!

I don't have any snake subs on the menu anytime soon, but I have developed a newfound respect and admiration for reptiles. Did you know that snakes were reptiles? Can you think of some other animals, like snakes, that reside in the reptiles class?

Your responses do not cease to amaze Ulysses and me. We are so proud of you! Reptiles include animals like turtles, lizards, crocodiles, alligators, and snakes. These creatures are cold-blooded, just like the fish we chatted about a few weeks ago. On a sunny day, you can find them hanging out on logs or rocks, warming themselves up.

Reptiles are also covered in scales, instead of fur like mammals or feathers like birds. These scales help to protect and waterproof the reptile. And in the case of snakes, scales help them slither along the ground. The fastest snake in the world is the Black Mamba, but it is also one of the most venomous, so you definitely don't want to race this one!

Reptiles lay eggs, just like birds do. However, most of their eggs are soft and leathery, which makes it easier for the baby snakes to hatch. After all, they don't have beaks to use to crack out of the shell.

I could go on for hours, but instead I want to see your reptilian moves. Check out the reptile pics below and see if you can move just like they do! (*Hint – Snakes slither across the ground, lizards walk on all fours, and turtles use their flippers to push across the land or through the water.*)

Reptiles, like snakes and lizards, are cold-blooded.

Reptilian Location

Location	Temperature
Inside	
Outside in Full Sun	
Outside in Shade	

Fingerprint Snakes

Unit 1: Animals Lab Manual - Week 3 Reptiles

Summer's Lab Presents: Insects

Creepy crawlies! That's what we are taking a look at this week!

I will be the first to admit that the thought of a pita pocket with spinach, tomatoes, and some honey-roasted ants makes me more than a little squeamish! But many people around the world eat bugs, like ants, locusts, and grasshoppers.

Ulysses says it is because insects are a great source or protein, but I suspect that it is because there are more insects on the Earth than any other creature! Insects live in every region and every habitat in the world.

Insects are part of a group of animals known as invertebrates. This means that they have do not have a backbone like fish and humans do. Can you think of some of the insects you can find in your area?

Once again, your brilliance at this age does not disappoint! Now, I do have to point out that spiders are not insects. Those guys all have eight legs, and insects only have six legs.

Insects also have a pair of antennae and a body made of three parts. These parts are known as the head, or front part with the antennae; the thorax, or middle part; and the abdomen, or back part. Some insects also have wings, which always come in pairs, one on each side of the thorax.

OK, it is your turn . . . can you point out each insect's six legs and antennae?

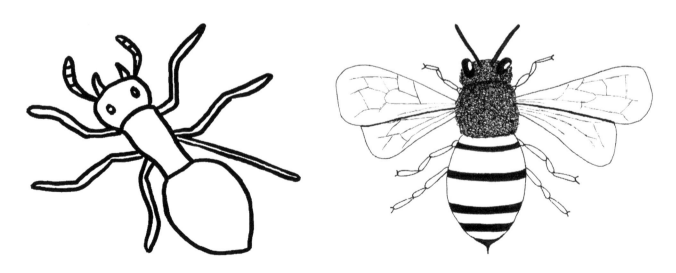

Insects, like ants, have six legs and a pair of antennae.

Attracting Ants

Type of Food	Were the ants attracted to it?

Shape Insects

SUMMER'S LAB

Unit 2: Humans

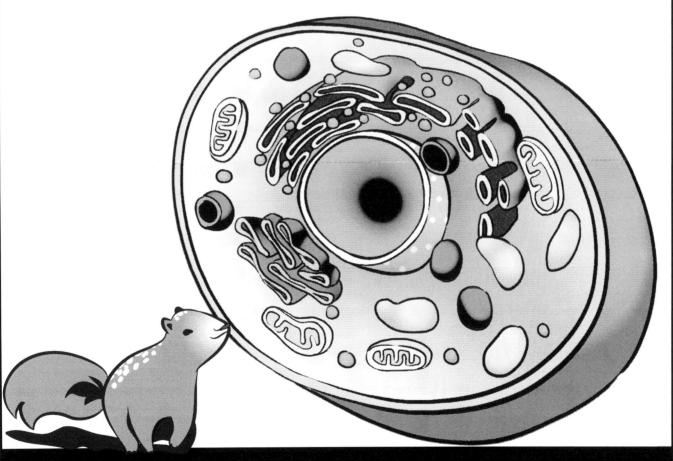

Student Lab Manual

Summer's Lab Presents: Living Things

Crunchy peanut butter and jelly on Wonder white bread - it always brings me back to childhood and the edible rocks we made! Delicious!! But we are not here to chat about rocks, we'll do that another time. Rocks are not living, and today we are here to discuss things that are living.

But before we do that, why don't you tell your teacher one thing that you know is living.

Whew - you got that one right! All around us, we can find both living and nonliving things. And the way we tell which is which is that all living things have the characteristics of life.

This means that a living thing develops, changes, and grows. All living things reproduce to make exact copies of themselves or offspring that are similar. Living things are also able to move as they respond and adapt to their environments.

Humans are living things. I am a living thing. Ulysses is a living thing. Your teacher is a living thing. You are a living thing and so is your class pet!

On the other hand, nonliving things do not show the characteristics of life. They may appear to show one or more of the same characteristics, but they do not show them all. Rocks and peanut butter are examples of non-living things.

Take a look at the pics below and see if you can tell which is living and which is non-living!

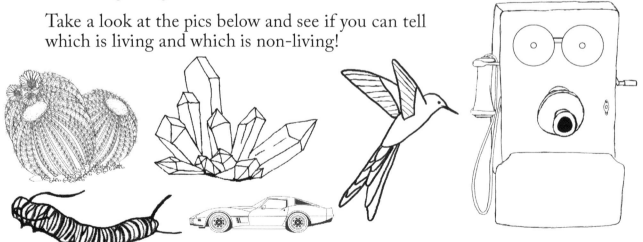

Unit 2: Humans Lab Manual - Week 1 Living Things

A living thing can adapt, change, develop, grow, and reproduce.

Living or Nonliving

Object Name	Does the object change, develop, or grow?	Does the object reproduce?	Does the object need food?	Does it move?	Does the object adapt or respond what is around it?	Living or Nonliving

Unit 2: Humans Lab Manual – Week 1 Living Things

Life Collage

UNIT 2: HUMANS LAB MANUAL - WEEK 1 LIVING THINGS

Summer's Lab Presents: Mammals

Mammals – this is the group of animals that you all will be most familiar with. Why, you ask? Because you are one of them! Did you know that humans are mammals? And so are arctic ground squirrels like Ulysses!

It turns out that you have more in common with your pet pooch than you think! Can you think of a few things that a pet dog, kitty cat, or lab-assistant squirrel have in common with you?

Wow, those are some great ideas. Ulysses pointed out that he, the kitty, and your pooch all have tails. Thankfully, that is not one of the common features of mammals. Can you imagine your parents running around with furry tails tagging along behind them?

Seriously, all mammals feed their young with milk. Momma rabbits, cats, dogs, squirrels, kangaroos, and humans provide this special, super-nutritious white liquid to their babies until they are old enough to eat their own food.

The other thing that all mammals have in common is that we are covered in fur or hair. And that fur or hair works hard to help keep us warm. You see mammals are warm-blooded, meaning that we trap and produce the heat we need to stay at just the right temperature.

Now, pull out your magnifying glass and see if you can count the number of hairs on your arm!

Mammals, like rabbits and humans, have fur or hair.

Mammal Comparison Chart

Name of Animal			
Size			
Skin Covering			
Ears and Eyes			
Arms and Legs			
Alike or Different			

Unit 2: Humans Lab Manual - Week 2 Mammals

Mammal Collage

Unit 2: Humans Lab Manual - Week 2 Mammals

Summer's Lab Presents: Body Cells

Every time I make an olive loaf sandwich – I prefer mine on French bread with a few slices of tomato and a quick swipe of mayochup, which is a super delicious ketchup and mayonnaise spread.

But I digress, back to the olive loaf…

Every time I see a slice of olive loaf, it makes me think of cells, not the battery-kind or the room-kind, but the life-kind. Before I share a bit more about what I mean, what do you know about cells?

That is fantastic! The cell is the basic building block of all living things, including our bodies.

Even though they are tiny, they are little powerhouses! Cells are responsible for all kinds of jobs. They can send messages, fight off germs, and turn food into energy.

All our body cells have a membrane that holds everything together. They are filled with gel-like liquid called cytoplasm. And nestled in the cytoplasm are different pieces, called organelles, that help the cell to do its job. One type of organelle, called mitochondria, looks like a kidney bean and helps to release energy.

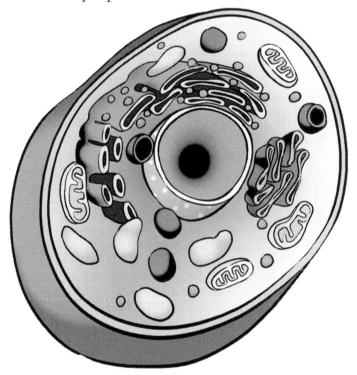

At the center of the cell is the olive, I mean the nucleus! The nucleus acts as the control center for the cell. Okay, now that you know a bit about cells, can you, with the help of your teacher, point out some of the things we just discussed on the picture of the cell?

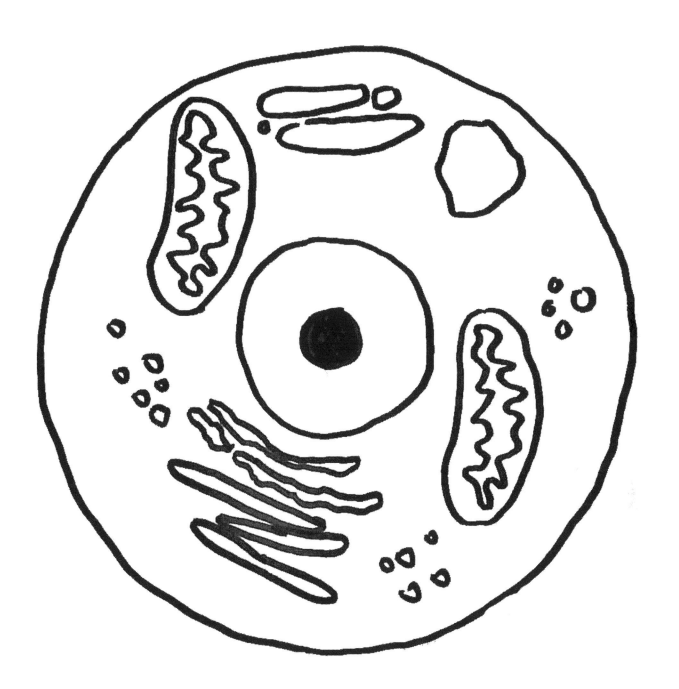

The cell is the basic building block of the body.

Unit 2: Humans Lab Manual - Week 3 Body Cells

Jell-O Cell

I learned that:

_____

_____

_____

_____

_____

_____

Unit 2: Humans Lab Manual – Week 3 Body Cells

Crafty Cell

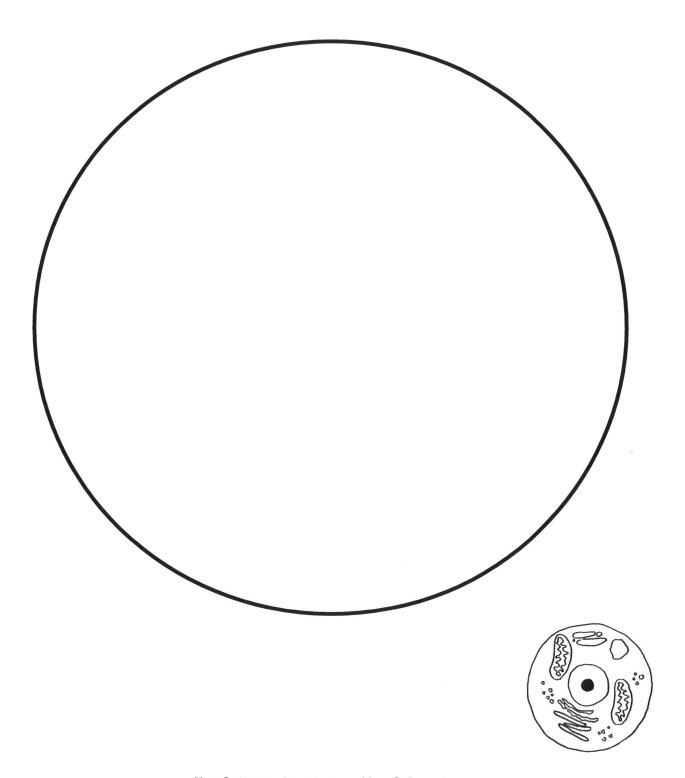

UNIT 2: HUMANS LAB MANUAL - WEEK 3 BODY CELLS

Summer's Lab Presents: Human Body

A good sandwich is composed of several parts that work together to provide a superb dining experience. Take the humble shrimp po-boy – tiny, crunchy, but juicy shrimp mix with cool lettuce, flavorful remoulade sauce, and the perfect crisp, but soft, French bread.

Each part of the sandwich plays a role in making the shrimp po-boy irresistible to Ulysses and me! How does this relate to the human body? I'll get to that in a moment, but before I do, what do you know about the human body?

Great answers! Let's chat about this sandwich-body relationship.

The human body, just like a good sandwich, is composed of many systems. These systems have structures, called organs, each with their own job. And these organs are made from tissues, which are composed of the very cells we chatted about last week!

Let's look at the digestive system, which is responsible for breaking down your food into bits your body can use for energy. Your teeth, esophagus, stomach, small intestines, and large intestines all work to break down food and absorb nutrients as the morsels you eat pass through these organs. They work together in a system, along with a few other organs, to turn those sandwiches into fuel for your body!

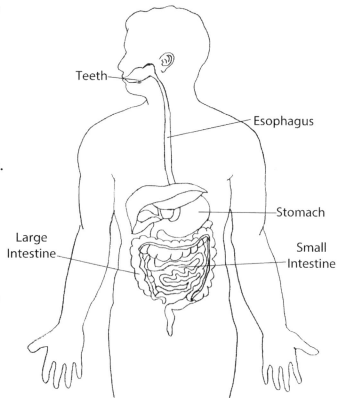

Okay, now it's your turn – take a moment to marvel at and observe the largest organ on your body, your skin! The skin, along with the hair, nails, and several glands, are parts of the integumentary system.

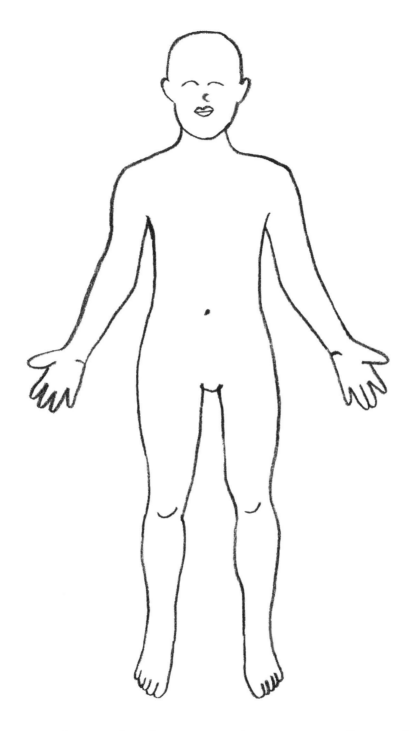

The human body is made up of systems that have organs, each with their own job.

Unit 2: Humans Lab Manual - Week 4 The Human Body

Model Stomach

I learned that:

_____

_____

_____

_____

_____

_____

Unit 2: Humans Lab Manual – Week 4 The Human Body

Body Organization

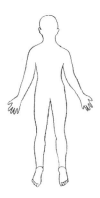

Unit 2: Humans Lab Manual - Week 4 The Human Body

SUMMER'S LAB

Unit 3: Plants

Student Lab Manual

Summer's Lab Presents: Plants

Ulysses and I love plants, but since the area around our lab is often covered in snow . . . I haven't yet mentioned that our lab is underground in Alaska, have I?

Well it is. And because of that, we have an indoor greenhouse with grow lights to test out our plant experiments.

Plants are super important for sustaining life on Earth, but before we get to that – let me ask you a question. What do you know about plants?

Wowzers – we haven't even started learning about plants and you already know all that! Super impressive!

Plants use light, water, and air to make food. We call the process plants use to make food photosynthesis. Which basically means "light" is "putting together." Kinda funny, eh?

Plants use light from the sun as energy. And a little substance inside the leaves, called chlorophyll, takes the energy and changes the nutrients the plant absorb into food it can use to grow. The chlorophyll is also the part that give the leaf its green color.

So, since plants need light to make food, they typically grow toward the light. But the super cool thing about plants is that in the process of creating the food they need, these plants give off oxygen, which we need to survive!

We are going to spend the next few weeks going over the different parts of the plant, so for now I will just leave you with a picture of one of my favorites, the crocus!

Plants grow toward the light.

Unit 3: Plants Lab Manual - Week 1 Plants

Plant Growth

Inches	Week 1	Week 2	Week 3	Week 4
18				
17				
16				
15				
14				
13				
12				
11				
10				
9				
8				
7				
6				
5				
4				
3				
2				
1				

Mosaic Plant

Summer's Lab Presents: Flowers

I love flowers! Especially when they are a part of a bouquet given to me by the dreamy Cecil Sassafras.

My favorite flower, as you already know, is the crocus, which comes in purple, white, or yellow. It's not the best flower to pick and put on your table, but there is nothing like seeing the Alaskan tundra covered with crocus blooms!

Before we dig into learning about flowers, can you tell me what you already know about the blooming structure of a plant?

Yes, that is so true! You are brilliant! Flowers come in all shapes, sizes, and colors. Most of them smell delicious, but some, like the corpse flower, smell like rotting flesh. All flowers give off a scent and have pretty-colored petals to attract pollinators, which is the main job of this part of the plant.

Flowers are the reproductive part of a plant. The blooms have all the right parts to produce a seed with a bit of help from an insect or from the wind.

All flowers begin as buds, which are tightly compacted. The bud blooms, or opens up, to reveal the parts of the flower. First there are petals, the brightly-colored blades that help to attract insects toward the center of the flower. In the center of the flower, we find the parts that work together to make a seed—the pistil, the anther, and the pollen. Pollinators move the pollen from the anthers, the shorter structures, to the pistil, the tall structure in the middle. We call this process pollination!

OK, your turn! Can you, with the help of your teacher, find the petals, pistil, and anther on the flowers?

Flowers are the reproductive part of a plant.

UNIT 3: PLANTS LAB MANUAL – WEEK 2 FLOWERS

Flower Dissection

What I observed in my flower:

_____
_____
_____
_____
_____
_____

Unit 3: Plants Lab Manual - Week 2 Flowers

Field of Flowers

Summer's Lab Presents: Seeds

Hot ham and cheese on multi-grain bread with whole grain mustard! It's one of the seed-packed sandwiches that inspired today's chat.

Multi-grain bread is packed with tiny seeds that are super good for your digestive tract—grains like quinoa, oats, and sunflower seeds. They make the bread super yummy.

But we are not here in the lab today to chat about bread! We are here to talk about seeds. Before I share some of what I know, can you tell me what you know about seeds?

Once again, you do not disappoint! I am so happy to be able to share my lab with someone like you for this year!!

Let's get down to business! Last week, we talked about flowers and about how they contain all the parts needed to make a seed. This week, we are going to learn about that seed!!

Seeds contain a teeny, tiny baby plant that just needs the right amount of water and warmth to sprout and grow into a big mama (or dada) plant. Most of what is inside the seed is food. The baby plant needs all these food stores to have the energy to grow roots and leaves so that it can start making its own food.

But up at the top (or side – depending upon which way you are holding your seed), there's a little bulge. That little knobby is the very beginning of a plant, and we have a very special name for it. It's called a cotyledon, which basically means seed leaf.

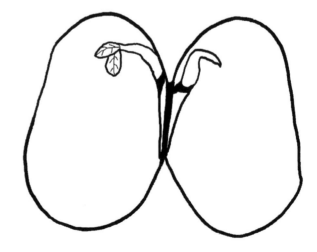

And one day, that little seed leaf will grow into the roots and leaves of a big plant! OK, your turn! Can you, with the help of your teacher, find the part of the seed that will become the plant in the diagram?

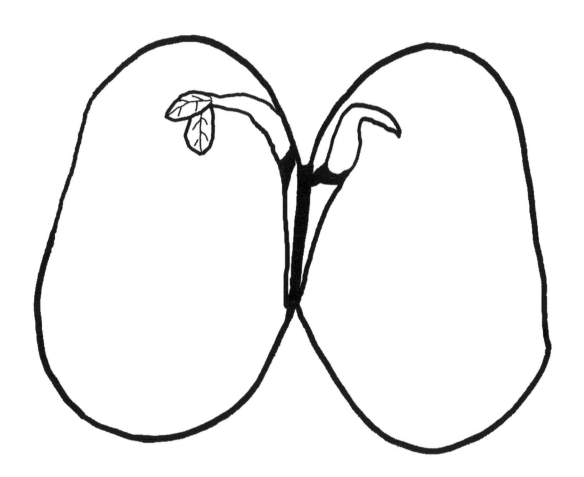

Seeds contain tiny baby plants.

Always Up

Seed	Which way it grew
#1	
#2	
#3	

I learned that:

_____

_____

_____

_____

_____

Unit 3: Plants Lab Manual – Week 3 Seeds

Apple Prints

Summer's Lab Presents: Trees

I love a good cheese and apple sandwich with mustard on whole grain bread, but what really takes a sandwich like that over the top is to eat it under the very tree that the apple came from! I love leaning back on the trunk and looking up at the crown of the tree laden with apples. The cool breezes drifting around us lead to the best post-lunch naps.

But we are not here to talk about naps today. We are here to chat about trees! Can you tell me what you know about trees?

Ahhhmazing! Trees can be either deciduous, meaning that they shed or lose their leaves in certain seasons, or evergreen, meaning that their leaves stay green year-round. The apple tree we sit under is a deciduous tree. The tree flowers in the spring and then the fruit develops and grows through the summer. In the fall, we harvest the apples just before the leaves turn colors and fall off.

But most of the trees around our lab are evergreen. These trees have needles that stick around all year long. And instead of the typical flowers and fruits, evergreen trees reproduce using cones.

Despite those differences, all trees have a few common parts. They all have a tough woody stem, called a trunk, that thickens as the tree grows older. From the trunk, the tree divides into branches, which form the crown of the tree. Under the ground, the tree has a huge root system that holds it in place.

OK, your turn! Can you, with the help of your teacher, find the parts of the tree – the trunk, the roots, and the crown – on the tree in the picture?

Trees are large plants with woody stems called trunks.

Unit 3: Plants Lab Manual - Week 4 Trees

Backyard Bark

Unit 3: Plants Lab Manual - Week 4 Trees

Tree Sculpture

Unit 3: Plants Lab Manual - Week 4 Trees

SUMMER'S LAB

Unit 4: Weather

Student Lab Manual

Summer's Lab Presents: The Sun

Ulysses and I just got back from this amazing little sandwich shack, called the Solar Shack, where they serve all kinds of sunny treats. But my favorite by far is the sun-dried tomato grilled cheese on sourdough bread.

Lunch just doesn't get much better than that, especially when you consider how much work goes into a sandwich that sounds so simple.

But we are not here to discuss how to make sun-dried tomatoes! We are here to chat about the sun. Before we do that, can you tell me where the sun is?

Yep! The sun appears up in our sky, but it's really way out at the center of our solar system. The sun has a very special job to do – it gives light and heat to the Earth. That's why it usually warmer during the day than it is at night when the sun is not shining on our part of the globe. This heat from the sun makes life as we know it possible on the Earth!

When an object, like a tree or a cloud, blocks out the rays of the sun, a shadow is created. And that shadow provides some much-needed shade on a hot day. In the shade, the light and heat from the sun's rays is diminished, so it feels a bit cooler on a sunny summer day.

Now it's your turn. Can you point out the sun in the picture? How about the shadow? On a hot sunny day, point to where you would want to set up your picnic.

Heat from the sun makes life possible on the Earth.

UNIT 4: WEATHER LAB MANUAL - WEEK I THE SUN

Solar Changes

What I observed:

_____

_____

_____

_____

_____

_____

Tissue Paper Sun

Unit 4: Weather Lab Manual - Week 1 The Sun

Summer's Lab Presents: Clouds

There is nothing more relaxing than wrapping up a good picnic with a game of cloud shapes. You know – the game where you lie back and look up, guessing the shapes that the clouds are forming.

Ulysses always comes up with the most interesting ideas. But today, we are not talking about cloud shapes; we are going to chat about what makes clouds. Before I do that, can you tell me what you know about clouds?

Brilliant! Clouds are made from tiny drops of water, called water vapor, in the sky. They form when warm air filled with these micro drops cools down.

The way a cloud looks depends upon how much water is in it and how fast it forms. If the cloud forms slowly, it will spread out in sheets. If the cloud forms quickly, it puff up into heaps, like marshmallows!

There are three main types of clouds, which are based on where you find them. Cirrus clouds are high and wispy. Alto clouds are mid-level clouds that can be puffy or flat. Stratus clouds form low, flat layers closest to the ground. There are also cumulus clouds, which are tall, puffy clouds that can grow and form between the layers.

Aren't clouds cool? Okie, dokie, now it's your turn – take a look at the clouds in the picture. How are they the same? How are they different?

Unit 4: Weather Lab Manual – Week 2 Clouds

Clouds are made from water vapor in the sky.

Unit 4: Weather Lab Manual – Week 2 Clouds

Cloudy Observations

Fluffy Clouds

Unit 4: Weather Lab Manual - Week 2 Clouds

Summer's Lab Presents: Weather

Once, while visiting a friend's lab, Ulysses and I went to this restaurant called the Hurricane Grill and they had the best Blue Cheese Bacon Burger I have ever tasted on that side of the Mississippi!

Thankfully, while we were there, no hurricanes were forecasted, but we did have a few rainstorms, which brings me to our topic for today – weather!

But before I share what I know, can you share what you know about weather?

Cheers to your intellect! Weather is the word we use to describe what is happening in the atmosphere, or rather in the air and sky outside.

It can be foggy.

It can be sunny and hot.

It can be breezy or windy.

It can be cloudy and cool.

It can be raining. It can be snowing.

It can be . . . well, you get my point! There are lots of options when it comes to the weather.

There's a whole branch of science devoted to predicting the weather. And meteorologists work hard to share with us what the weather will be, but sometimes the weather just seems to have a mind of its own!

Okay, now it's your turn! Find a window and look outside, up at the sky. What is today's weather?

Unit 4: Weather Lab Manual - Week 3 Weather

Weather is what is happening outside in the sky.

Weather in a Jar

Time	My Observations
After 5 minutes	
After 10 minutes	
After 15 minutes	
After 20 minutes	
After 25 minutes	
After 30 minutes	

Weather Painting

Summer's Lab Presents: Seasons

Here in our Alaskan Lab, we get to experience all four seasons, but three of those are much shorter than they are in the lower 48. Winter is long, which is the reason Ulysses and I eat lots of hot sandwiches, like the Hot Brown.

Warm chunks of turkey topped with bacon and drizzled with Alfredo sauce. Slices of cool tomatoes and sandwiched between two toasted slices of country white – it's amazing! And certainly enough to keep you going on a cold winter day.

But we are not here to discuss the merits of a hot sandwich on a cold day – we are here to chat about the seasons. Before I continue, what do you know about the seasons?

Wow! Those are some great tidbits! A season is a collection of days with a typical weather pattern. On earth, we have four seasons – spring, summer, fall, and winter. Sometimes people refer to fall as autumn, but that's a whole 'nother ball of wax!

Typically, winter has shorter days that can be filled with cold temperatures and snow. Around spring, it warms up and the flowers begin to bloom. During summer, the days are longer and hotter. And finally, fall comes along with a drop in the temperature and a change in the leaves, which leads us back into winter all over again!

Winter, spring, summer, and fall are all seasons, and each one typically sees a change in the weather. Okay, now it's your turn – can you guess what season it is now?

Unit 4: Weather Lab Manual - Week 4 Seasons

Spring, summer, fall, and winter are all seasons.

Unit 4: Weather Lab Manual - Week 4 Seasons

Weather Watch

Day	Weather
1	
2	
3	
4	
5	

Unit 4: Weather Lab Manual – Week 4 Seasons

Seasons Collage

SUMMER'S LAB

Unit 5: Rocks

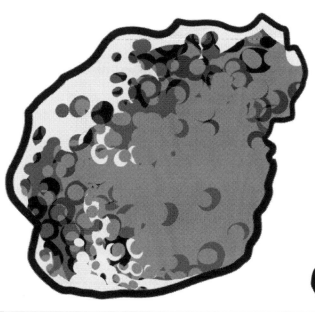

Student Lab Manual

Summer's Lab Presents: Rocks

When I was in school, my teacher taught us about layers in rock using a crunchy peanut butter and jelly sandwich that was mush until no human would want to eat it.

But you can relax, I shall not subject you to mushy sandwiches – unless it's a panini, because those are melty, delicious, crispy sandwich goodness. So, they don't really qualify as mushy sandwiches.

But there I go again – off on a sandwich tangent when we are supposed to be talking about rocks. Before we dig into that, can you tell me what you know about rocks?

Well, you just rolled through sharing that!

Seriously, rocks are … well … rocky. These hard, natural objects can be found all over the Earth's surface. There are many different types of rocks, and they have many different uses. Rocks are used to build buildings, to form statues, and to create clay pots.

Rocks come in all shapes and sizes, but all rocks are a mixture of minerals. There are three main types of rocks. First, there are sedimentary rocks, which are formed as layers of crushed minerals and the decayed remains of plants or animals. Second, there are metamorphic rocks, which are rocks that have been changed by heat or pressure. And finally, there are igneous rocks, which start as melted rock that cools to form rocks!

Now it's your turn. Can you guess which rock in the picture below is a sedimentary rock?

 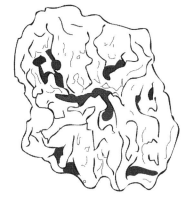 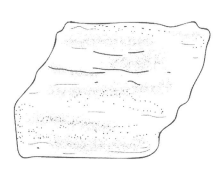

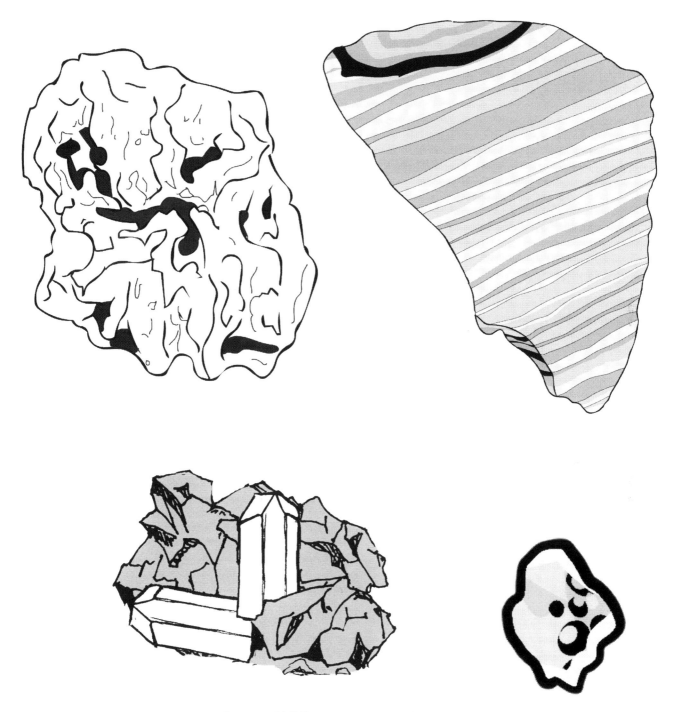

Rocks come in different shapes and sizes, but they are all a mixture of minerals.

UNIT 5: ROCKS LAB MANUAL - WEEK 1 ROCKS

Rock Hunt

I found:

_____
_____
_____
_____
_____
_____

Unit 5: Rocks Lab Manual – Week 1 Rocks

Rock Stamping

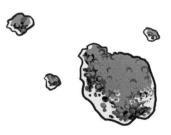

Unit 5: Rocks Lab Manual - Week 1 Rocks

Summer's Lab Presents: Mountains

I love a picnic lunch! Ulysses and I have this special spot we go to when we need to get out of the office for a sandwich-filled excursion. It's on a rocky outcrop and has an amazing view of the mountains.

We'd love for you to visit and share a sandwich or two with us there. You can bring your favorite lunch and we can swap science stories, but until then, how about you tell me what you already know about mountains?

That was very interesting!

Mountains are tall rocky bumps – or rather features – on the surface of the Earth. They can have steep sides called slopes. And the very tippy top of the mountain is called the summit. Some mountains are so tall that they have a point, called the tree line, where the trees no longer grow.

Mountains are found on every continent on the globe. And every large land mass on the Earth has a row of mountains called a range. Here in North America, where our lab is located, we have two major ranges – the Appalachians and the Rockies.

Now it's your turn. Can you point out the slopes, tree line, and summit on the mountains below?

Unit 5: Rocks Lab Manual - Week 2 Mountains

Mountains are tall, rocky bumps on the surface of the Earth.

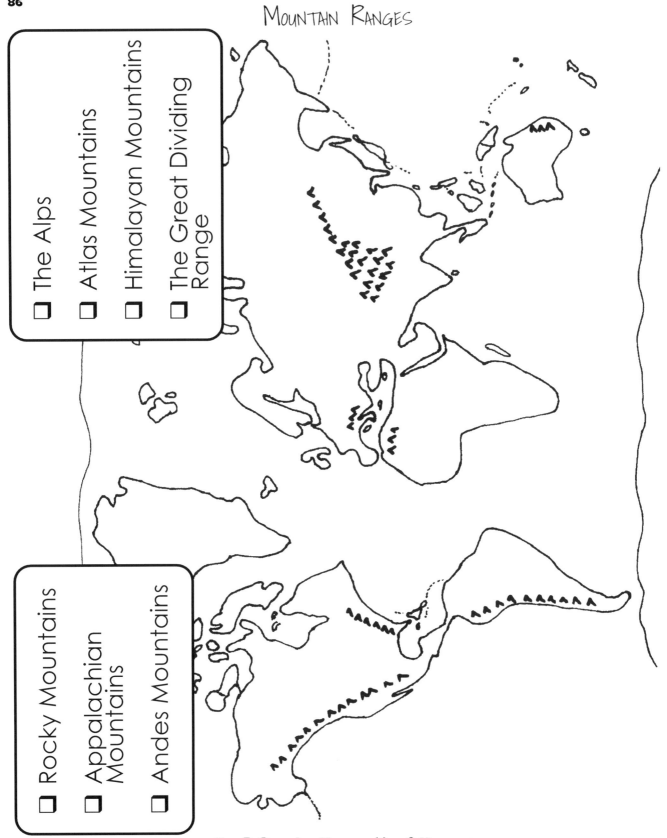

Torn Paper Mountain

Unit 5: Rocks Lab Manual - Week 2 Mountains

Summer's Lab Presents: Volcanoes

I love a good grilled cheese sandwich – the bread is crunchy, and the cheese is all melty. Yum!

But you know how the cheese sometimes oozes out of the place you just took a bite? That oozing always makes me think about volcanoes!

Why, you ask? Well, I'll tell you in just a moment. Before that, can you tell me what you know about volcanoes?

Wow – that is fascinating! Back to the cheese – the molten cheese to be more precise. The oozing cheese is melted, just like the rock that oozes or explodes out of a volcano. Thank goodness the cheese doesn't explode out of our sandwiches!!

Anywhoo, under what we can see of a volcano is a whole bunch of hot rock, called magma. This molten, or melted, rock comes from deep inside the Earth. When the magma gets too hot, pressure builds up, and eventually . . . BOOM!

The volcano blows its top or sometimes the magma just oozes out depending on how much pressure there is. But when this eruption happens, ash and hot, sticky rock spill out. And now that the magma that was inside the Earth is outside, we call it lava. And when the lava cools, it forms igneous rocks. How cool is that!

Volcanoes are found all over the world, including under the sea. And they come in all shapes and sizes, but the most recognizable shape in the cinder cone volcano, which you can see in the picture.

Volcanoes explode hot, sticky rock from inside the Earth.

Toothpaste Volcano

I saw that:

_____
_____
_____
_____
_____
_____

Unit 4: Weather Lab Manual - Week 3 Weather

Volcanic Art

Summer's Lab Presents: Fossils

So, do you remember that teacher I told you about at the beginning of our chat about rocks? The only who mushed the humble PB&J sandwich for science?

Well, she also thought it was a good idea to smash gummy bears in bread to teach us about fossils – she obviously did not love a good sandwich as much as Ulysses and I do.

I still shudder at the memory of that glistening gummy impression in some of the finest sourdough bread our little town offered.

But I digress. We are not here to chat about my old school memories; we are here to learn about fossils and before we do that, can you tell me what you know about fossils?

You never fail to impress!! We find fossils in rocks all over the Earth. They are the remains of plants or animals that died many years ago.

When these living things died, they got stuck in the mud, and as time went by, more mud pressed on top of them. Eventually, there was so much weight that the mud turned into rock.

Over time, the living thing disappeared or decayed. All that was left was the imprint, or impression, of that plant or animal, on the rock.

Now it's your turn. Can you guess what made the imprints on the fossils in the picture?

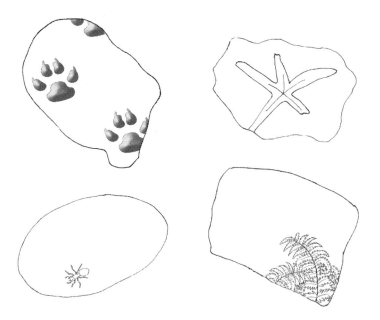

Unit 4: Weather Lab Manual - Week 4 Seasons

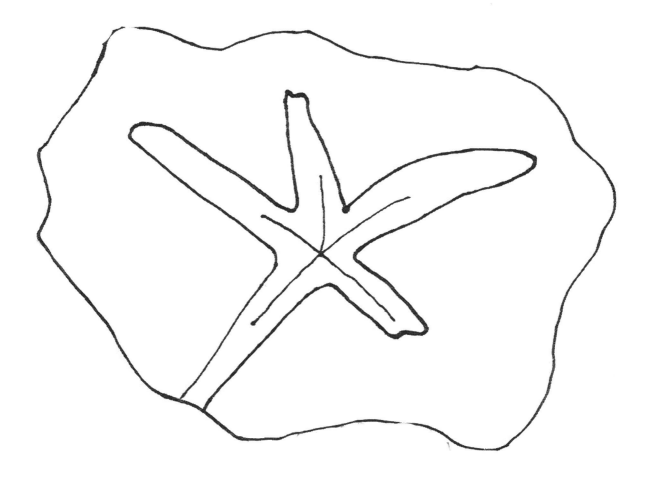

Fossils are imprints of long-gone plants or animals.

Impression Fossil

I saw that:

_____

_____

_____

_____

_____

Unit 4: Weather Lab Manual – Week 4 Seasons

Fossilized Art

Unit 4: Weather Lab Manual - Week 4 Seasons

SUMMER'S LAB

Unit 6: Space

Student Lab Manual

Summer's Lab Presents: The Moon

Cheese. Any good sandwich maker knows that a good cheese can make all the difference.

And so maybe it was some crazy deli-owner who started the rumor that the moon was made of cheese. Maybe that was part of his plan to get people to try his sandwiches.

I don't know, but Ulysses and I do know that the moon is not made of cheese. It's made of . . . wait, before I share that – what do you know about the moon?

Wow, that's interesting info! Did you know that the moon our closest space-neighbor? It goes around, or orbits, the Earth in the same way that the Earth orbits the Sun. It takes about 27 days to go around the Earth.

As the moon moves, parts of it are "lit" by the sun, which makes the moon look like it is a shining beacon in the night sky. The moon also appears to be changing shape night after night. We call these different shapes phases, and the pattern they follow the lunar cycle.

It all starts with a full moon. Then, the moon appears as if it is disappearing or waning until it gets all swallowed up in darkness. This is called the new moon and after that happens, the moon starts appearing, or waxing, until it gets to a full moon and the cycle starts all over again!

Now it's your turn. Can you point out below the full moon and the new moon? Can you show where the moon is waning (disappearing) and where it is waxing (appearing)?

The moon orbits the Earth and can be seen in the night sky.

Unit 6: Space Lab Manual – Week 1 Moon

Moon Cookies

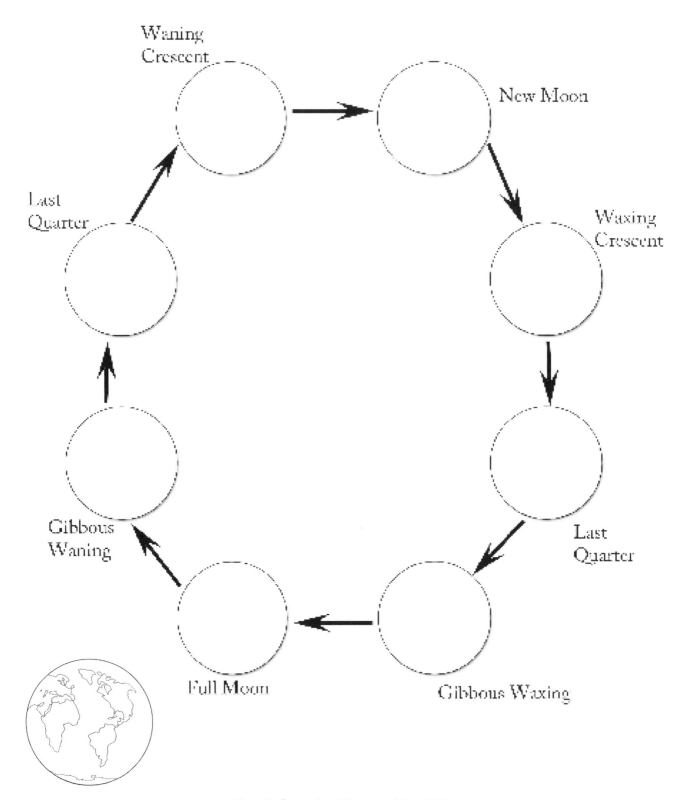

Unit 6: Space Lab Manual - Week 1 Moon

Moon Model

Unit 6: Space Lab Manual - Week 1 Moon

Summer's Lab Presents: Astronauts

Did you know that there is no bread in space? That means that my dear friend and astronaut can't have a single sandwich while he is on the International Space Station.

It's a tough life for those guys. But when he gets back, Ulysses and I make him a giant Reuben sandwich – complete with corned beef and sauerkraut, dripping with melted Swiss and Russian dressing. He gobbles up that rye bread encased deliciousness like a starving man in the desert!

But we are not here to discuss an astronaut's sandwich preferences! We are here to talk about what astronauts do, but before I share – what do you think an astronaut does?

Wow – that's an interesting job description! Astronauts are people who train for years and years so that they can take part in missions to space. Their job is to help us learn more about the universe. Sometimes they are in space for only a few days to do a quick repair job; sometimes they live in space for weeks to do research on the International Space Station.

Either way, when astronauts are in space, they have to wear a special space suit. These days, the space suit has a visor that protects their eyes from the sun, which is super strong out in space. It has places to attach the tools they need and a camera to record what they are doing. The space suit has a backpack with oxygen for breathing and water to help heat or cool the astronaut. It is made of many layers of fabric that help keep the astronaut safe and allow him or her to move about in space.

With all this stuff, the space suit is super heavy! It weighs around 300 pounds when it's all there, but that's okay because out in space, the astronaut is weightless, thanks to a lack of gravity.

Now it's your turn. Can you tell me about the kind of space suit you would design?

An astronaut is a person who travels to space.

Space Materials

Fabric	Temperature after 15 minutes in the refrigerator
Thick Fabric	Hot Warm Cold
Thin Fabric	Hot Warm Cold
No Fabric	Hot Warm Cold

Spacesuit Design

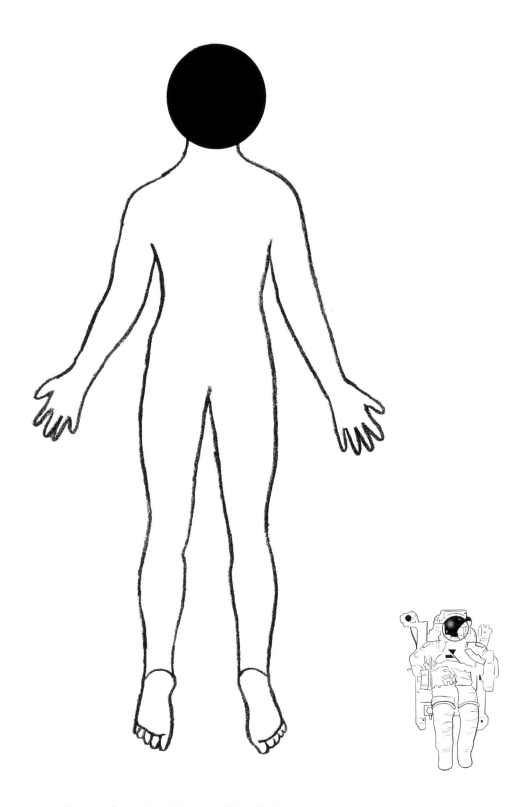

Unit 6: Space Lab Manual - Week 2 Astronauts

Summer's Lab Presents: Our Solar System

So, remember last week, when I said there was no bread in space? Well, there once was a sandwich in space! A long time ago, an astronaut from the *Gemini 3* mission thought it would be a good idea to smuggle his favorite sandwich into space in his flight suit.

Once out there, he took a out and it turned out to be not quite as delectable in outer space as it was on Earth. It turned out to cause quite the hullabaloo and a lot of today's space cuisine rules are there because of that single corned-beef-sandwich smuggle.

But we are not here to discuss space food; we are here today to talk about the solar system. Before I share some cool facts, can you tell me what you know about our solar system?

Alrighty then! Our solar system is located on an arm of the Milky Way galaxy. It is the collection of planets and other objects that orbit around the sun, which is at the very center.

Our solar system has eight major planets – Mercury, Venus, Earth, Mars, Jupiter, Saturn, Uranus, and Neptune – and several dwarf planets, including Pluto. Pluto was once considered a planet, until astronomers came together and created a better definition of what a planet is – it caused quite the uproar back in my day.

Our solar system also includes comets, stars, asteroids, and any other kind of space debris, like satellites, that orbit around the sun. To us here on Earth, our solar system seems huge. But really, it's one small part of a galaxy that is one small part of a massive universe!

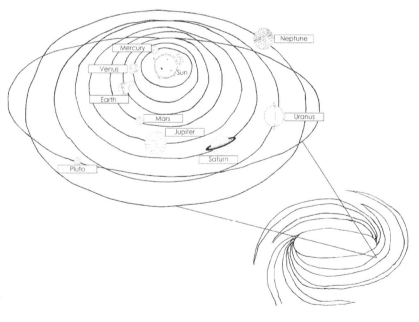

Now it's your turn. Can you point out the sun in our solar system? Remember, it's at the center. Can you point to one of the planets? Which one do you think is Earth?

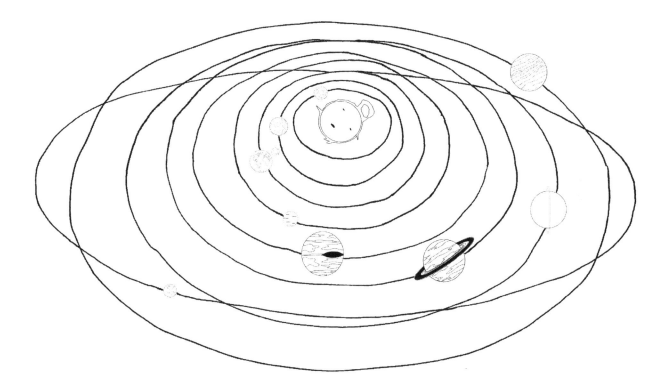

Our solar system includes a group of planets and other objects all in orbit around the Sun.

Unit 6: Space Lab Manual - Week 3 Our Solar System

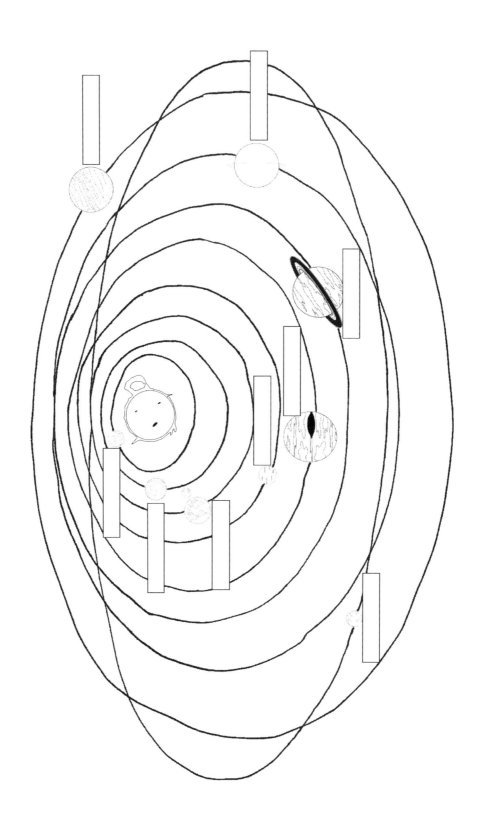

Galaxy Art

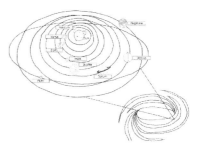

Unit 6: Space Lab Manual - Week 3 Our Solar System

Summer's Lab Presents: Stars

On a clear night, Ulysses and I like to take our French dip sandwiches outside. The warm roast beef and melted cheese blend with the savory beef consommé as we enjoy an incredible scene.

We dunk until our hearts are content, staring up at the pictures painted on the canvas of the night sky. It's as close as we get to visiting a museum during our busier times.

There is peace in filling your belly with a simple, warm meal as you gaze at the same stars people have been looking at for hundreds of years. But we are not here to chat about how Ulysses and I unwind – we are here to talk about constellations.

What do you know about constellations or stars?

You are one smart cookie! When we look up at the night sky, all those white dots we see are stars. Stars are really giant balls of exploding gas, but they are so far away from us that they look like tiny, pinpricks of light. The closest star to our planet is actually the sun!

In the days before GPS and maps on our phones, people used to use the stars to navigate or find their way. To make this easier, they gave groups or patterns in the stars, names. These constellations were named after heroes, animals, and other familiar objects.

Today, we have 88 named constellations, or groups of stars that form pictures in the sky. Some are easy to spot, like the Big Dipper and Orion's belt. Some are a bit harder to find, like Cygnus the Swan, which you see on your sheet. But the longer you observe, the more you will see!

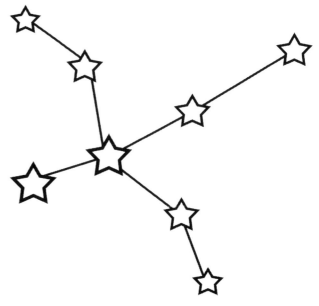

Now it's your turn. Have you ever seen a star picture, otherwise known as a constellation, in the night sky?

Unit 6: Space Lab Manual – Week 4 Stars

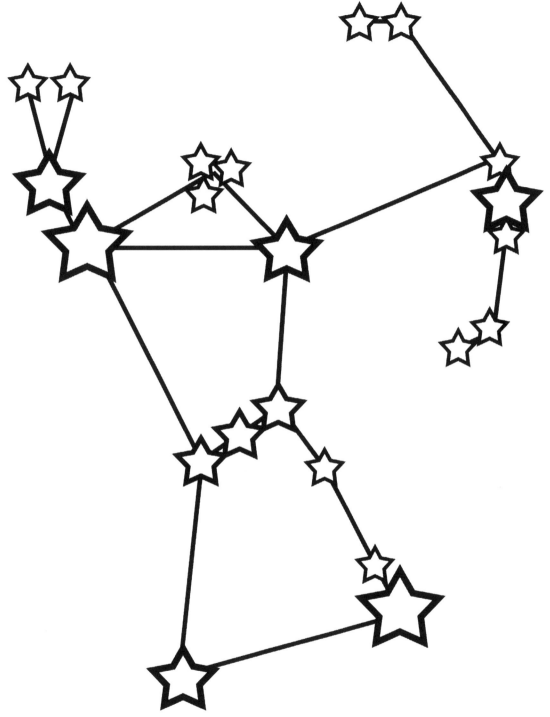

Stars form pictures in the sky called constellations.

Flashlight Planetarium

I saw that:

_____

_____

_____

_____

_____

_____

Constellation Resist

Unit 6: Space Lab Manual - Week 4 Stars

SUMMER'S LAB

Unit 7: Matter

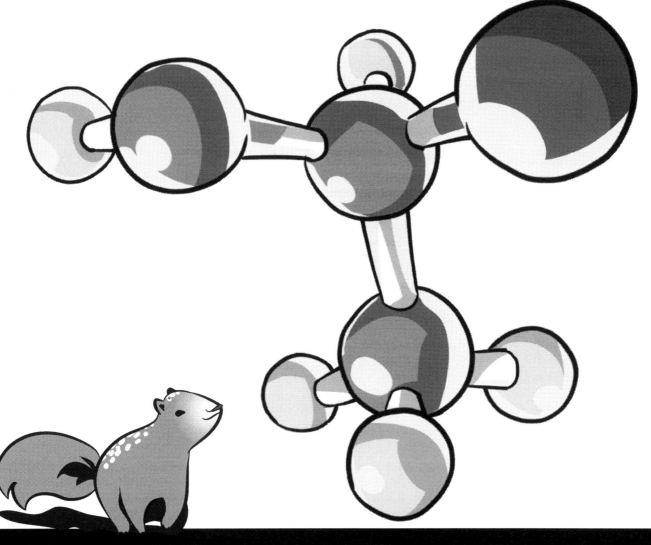

Student Lab Manual

Summer's Lab Presents: Atoms

One of my favorite snacks at teatime is a ham, brie, and apple finger sandwich. Ulysses prefers a peanut butter and bacon tea sandwich, which I haven't had the chutzpah to try . . . yet.

Anywhoo, these tiny sandwiches hit the spot when it comes to an afternoon snack. Each one contains all the important keys of a full sandwich, just in a smaller package. And right now, you are thinking "That's nice, but what in the world do tea sandwiches have to do with chemistry."

Well, quite a lot – but that's not the point. The point is that we are here today to chat about atoms, but before I share what I know, have you ever heard of an atom before?

Oh, fantastic! So, the tea sandwich is the smallest sandwich and the atom is the tiny unit that builds everything around us. See the connection? Yeah, it is a bit of a stretch . . . but seriously, the atom is super tiny! It's so small that you can't see it with your bare eyes. You have to use something that magnifies it, or rather makes it much, much bigger.

Even though scientists couldn't see atoms, the idea that they existed has been around for hundreds of years. They believed that all matter – in other words, everything – was composed of tiny particles and they called those specks atoms.

Nowadays, we know that atoms have a central core called a nucleus that contains protons and neutrons. And that atoms have electrons whizzing around the outside of the core. These electrons, protons, and neutrons are called subatomic particles.

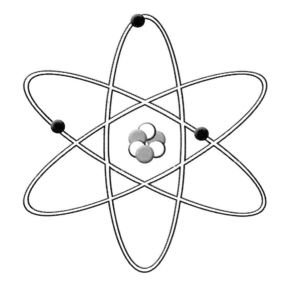

Atoms have an equal number of protons and electrons. If they don't, we call them ions. And typically, atoms of the same type will have the same number of protons and neutrons. If they don't, we call these isotopes!

Now it's your turn. Can you point out where you think the nucleus in the atom on the picture? Can you point out where you think the electrons are?

Unit 7: Matter Lab Manual - Week 1 Atoms

Atoms are the building blocks of matter.

Atom Model

My atom model:

Unit 7: Matter Lab Manual - Week 1 Atoms

Fingerprint Atom

Unit 7: Matter Lab Manual - Week 1 Atoms

Summer's Lab Presents: Liquids and Solids

Let's say you set a piece of bread on a plate and top it with a slice of bologna. Then, you unwrap a square of cheese and place it on the bologna. Maybe you add a bit of tomato or some mayonnaise before you cover it all with another piece of bread.

You step back and stare at the bologna sandwich on the plate in front of you. Does it move on its own? No, it does not.

And the reason for that can be explained with science! It all has to do with the states of matter, but before I explain all that – what do you know about liquids and solids?

Hmm, that is very interesting! Both liquids and solids are what we call states of matter. These are ways that matter, or things, can be. It has quite a bit to do with the movement of the atoms inside the object, but we won't get into all that right now.

Let's go back to your bologna sandwich, which is a solid. Your bologna has a first name, wait that's not right . . . your bologna sandwich will not move on its own. It stays in the same place you left it until you touch it again. This is because solids keep their shape.

Now let's say you have a glass of lemonade with your sandwich. And, oops, your clumsy sibling bumps your glass and it tips over. The lemonade spills everywhere! Why? Because lemonade is a liquid and liquids move, taking shape of the container they are in. When a liquid leaves a container, it spreads out everywhere, moving without any of your help.

That's a super simple way of looking at the two states of matter – solids and liquids. There are two more states – gas and plasma – but we'll save those for future studies.

For right now, it's your turn. Can you look at the picture and point to the solid ice? How about the liquid water?

Unit 7: Matter Lab Manual – Week 2 Liquids and Solids

Liquids can move,
but solids keep their shape.

UNIT 7: MATTER LAB MANUAL – WEEK 2 LIQUIDS AND SOLIDS

Is it liquid or solid?

Material	Is it liquid or solid?	
	Liquid	Solid
	Liquid	Solid
	Liquid	Solid
	Liquid	Solid
	Liquid	Solid
	Liquid	Solid

Liquid-Solid Collage

Unit 7: Matter Lab Manual - Week 2 Liquids and Solids

Summer's Lab Presents: Freezing and Melting

On a hot summer day, Ulysses and I like to wrap up our meal with an ice cream sandwich. Ulysses prefers the standard version, while I love a good Neapolitan ice cream sandwiches!

The only bad thing about ice cream sandwiches is that on a hot day you have to gobble them up fast ... well, maybe that's not such a bad thing! I bet you can tell me why ...

Yep! We have to gobble up our ice cream sandwiches on a hot day because if we don't, they will melt. And nobody likes a melty, mushy ice cream sandwich!

Well, our little hot-day-ice-cream snafu can be explained with science. You see, as the ice cream sandwich heats up, the tiny stuff inside, the stuff that makes up the ice cream, starts to heat up and move around faster. This causes our ice cream to go from a solid to a liquid and we call the process melting.

Now, let's say we realized our ice cream sandwich was starting to melt and ran inside to put it in the freezer. After about 10 minutes or so, we could pull it out and all the ice cream would be solid and firm once more. This is because, in the freezer, the tiny stuff inside cools down and basically stops moving. The ice cream in our sandwich has gone from a near liquid to a firm solid and we call this process freezing.

In short, melting is when a solid is heated up and turns into a liquid. Freezing is when a liquid is chilled and turns into solid.

Now it's your turn. Can you show me which way is melting? Can you show me which way is freezing?

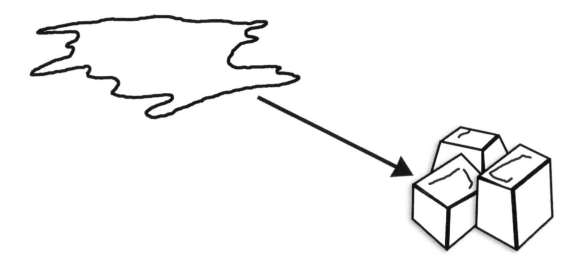

Freezing is when a liquid is chilled and turns into solid.

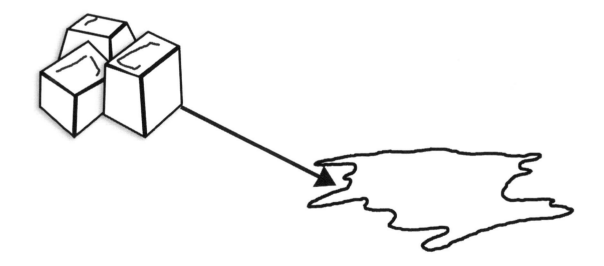

Melting is when a solid is heated up and turns into a liquid.

Changes in State

	My Observations
Frozen Water	
Melted Water	

I learned that:

_____

_____

_____

_____

_____

_____

Ice Paint

Unit 7: Matter Lab Manual – Week 3 Freezing and Melting

Summer's Lab Presents: Mixtures and Solutions

Hummus, roasted red peppers, and sprouts in a wrap. Ham and Swiss cheese on rye. Salami, provolone, and cucumbers on French bread.

All these sandwiches are a combination of delicious ingredients with a "breadish" delivery system. These sandwiches are not only tasty, they are mixtures.

The soda or lemonade you drink with your sandwich is special type of mixture called a solution. Before I explain what mixtures or solutions are, do you know anything about these?

Ahh, mixtures and solutions are big topics from chemistry. And after we finish today, you are going to be able to impress so many adults with your knowledge!

A mixture is a combination of solids, liquids, or gases – in other words, it's a combination of matter. Mixtures can be easily separated back into their original parts by sifting or filtering. But some mixtures, known as solutions, have substances dissolved in a liquid. These mixtures can be separated by evaporation.

Mixtures are easy to figure out, but for a solution let's think of how we make lemonade. You start by pouring some lemon juice, or if you are really industrious you squeeze a few lemons, into a pitcher. Then, you add a bit of sugar to the juice. You stir, stir, stir until the sugar crystals disappear. And to top it all off you add some water, creating some delicious lemonade. And my guess is that you had no idea that what you were making was a chemical solution!

Clear as muddy water? Which, by the way, is a another mixture - one that we can filter all that mud out of . . . eventually! Now it's your turn – grab a few lemons and a spot of sugar, or your favorite Kool-Aid powder, and mix up a solution! Or a bowl, some sand, and a few LEGO® bricks to make a mixture you can sift!

Unit 7: Matter Lab Manual - Week 4 Mixtures and Solutions

A mixture is a combination of solids or liquids. A solution is a mixture where a solid is dissolved in a liquid.

CRYSTAL SOLUTIONS

I saw that:

_____
_____
_____
_____
_____
_____

UNIT 7: MATTER LAB MANUAL - WEEK 4 MIXTURES AND SOLUTIONS

Solution Painting

Unit 7: Matter Lab Manual - Week 4 Mixtures and Solutions

SUMMER'S LAB

Unit 8: Energy

STUDENT LAB MANUAL

Summer's Lab Presents: Forces

Ulysses and I were outside one sunny afternoon having a picnic with our friends, who also happen to be teachers in a local school. I had prepared a delicious chicken salad, complete with almonds and a pinch of paprika – no celery or grapes for this gal!

Anywhoo, I had stuffed those French bread rolls so full of chicken salad that as soon as you picked one up and took a bite, a clump of the delicious concoction fell out the bottom.

And this action led to a discussion of forces with our friends, but before I share about that, what do you know about forces?

Interesting! You see, our sandwiches had no chicken salad motion on our plates. But as soon as we brought them up to our mouths, the force of gravity pulled a clump of the chicken salad from our sandwich down to the plate.

Every day, we encounter forces. These pushes and pulls cause motion or slow it down. Some of these forces we can see, like when we push a car or pull an object toward us. When we make a paper airplane and throw it into the air, the force of our push helps it to fly.

Some of these forces are invisible, like gravity, which pulls objects down toward the Earth, or friction, which slows an object down. We'll chat about another invisible force, magnetism, in a few weeks.

For now, I want you to remember that forces are pushes and pulls that transfer energy. And with that, it's your turn to practice using forces. First, make a paper airplane and then apply a push force to fly your creation.

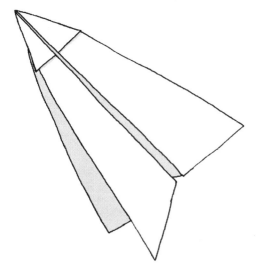

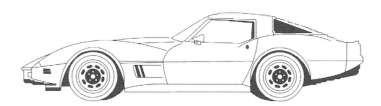

Unit 8: Energy Lab Manual – Week 1 Forces

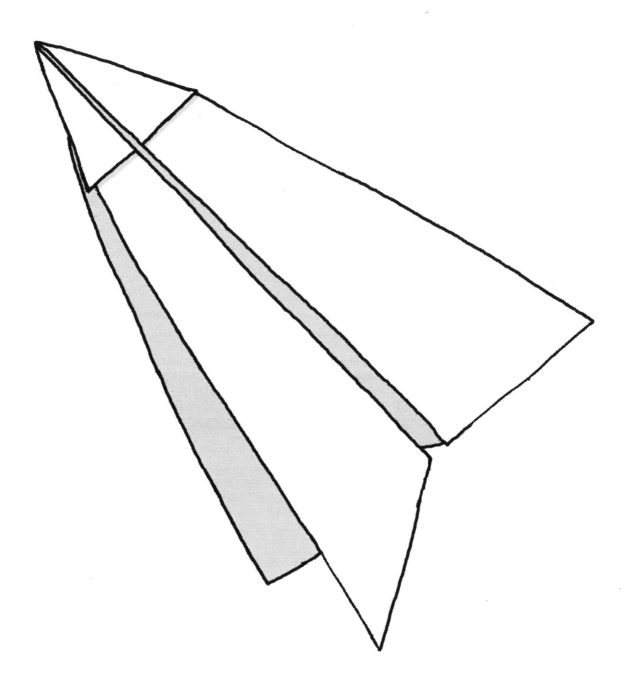

A force is a push or a pull that can cause motion or slow it down.

Push and Pull

	What the car did
On table	
After a push	
After a pull	

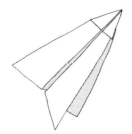

Unit 8: Energy Lab Manual – Week 1 Forces

Motion Painting

Summer's Lab Presents: Sound

We have a friend and family member who loves Flamin' Hot Cheetos. He loves them so much that he eats them out of the bag, dips them in ranch, and adds them to his peanut butter sandwich.

I have to say, it's not a sandwich that I want to try – I prefer jelly on peanut butter sandwiches. But it is one of the few sandwiches I know of that makes an amazing sound.

And sound is exactly what we are going to chat about today. But before I share, can you tell me what you know about sound?

Wow! I bet you can make some super silly sounds and we'll do just that in a few moments. The sounds we hear are actually vibrations, or waves, that travel through the air. When those waves reach us, our ears collect them and send the vibration-information to our brain. Our brains interpret that info into the sounds we hear. It's quite the amazing process!

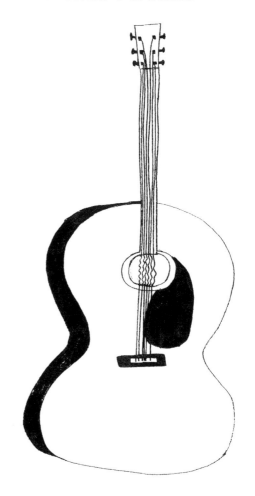

Sound waves can travel through the air, through solids, and through liquids, but the speed at which they travel can change depending on what the vibrations are moving through. That's why it sounds so weird when you try to talk to each other under the water!

The faster the sound waves move, the higher the pitch, or tone, sounds. And the closer the origination of the vibrations is to us, the louder the sound seems.

In short, sound is the movement of energy through something. Now that you understand a bit more about what sound is, it's your turn to make some noise. With your parent's or leader's permission, use your voice, hands, or feet to make some vibrations!

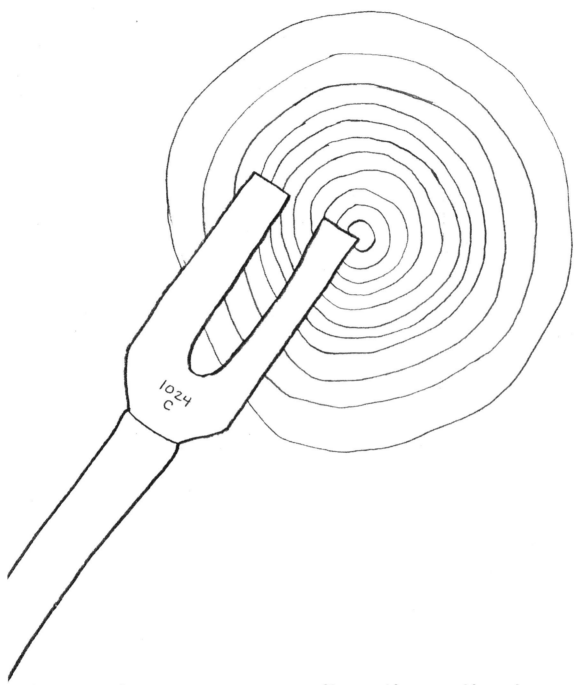

Sound waves are vibrations that can travel through the air.

Tonoscope

I saw that:

_____
_____
_____
_____
_____
_____

Plate Shaker

Summer's Lab Presents: Light

Glow-in-the-dark sandwiches – good idea or bad idea? One April Fool's Day, a McDonald's in India put out a meme with a glow-in-the-dark hamburger. It looked interesting, but very unappetizing.

Turns out, it was a gimmick and wasn't a real sandwich they were offering. Food doesn't make its own light; instead, light helps us to see those sandwiches on our plate.

But before I go into more about what light is, let's take a moment so you can share what you know about light.

Ahh, you never fail to surprise me! Light is basically energy. It's energy that bounces off of objects to that we can see them. Our eyes take in all that bouncing energy and send the information to our brainy parts. And our brains turn that info into the pictures we see.

The light can be split into different waves that represent the different colors of the rainbow. You know those right?

Right, Roy G. Biv – red, orange, yellow, green, blue, indigo, and violet. And this fact allows us to see different colors.

The sun is our greatest source of natural light, but we can also get light from candles, electronics, light bulbs, and stuff that glows-in-the-dark. Remember, when we block out the sun, or any other light source, we can create a shadow. This is a dark area when that takes the shape of the object that is blocking out the light!

Now it's your turn. Can you make a few shadow puppets on the way using your hands and a flashlight?

Light is energy that bounces off objects so we can see them.

LIGHT AND DARK

With the light on

With the light off

UNIT 8: ENERGY LAB MANUAL - WEEK 3 LIGHT

Color Mixing

Summer's Lab Presents: Magnets

I am a sandwich magnet, which, by now, you have probably already guessed. I always manage to find a new sandwich to try in every new place we visit, and I am rarely disappointed.

After all, is there a better meal delivery system than a sandwich? I think not. But we are not here to discuss the culinary merits of sandwiches.

We are here to discuss our last science sandwich together . . . sniff, sniff . . . this one is all about magnets. But before I share, what do you know about magnets?

Ahhh-mazing! I have so enjoyed your answers this year, and I will miss our little chats!! Magnets like to attract things, such as metal stuff and other magnets. The area around a magnet where it can attract things is called a magnetic field. Some materials are naturally magnetic, and some can be magnetized, meaning that we give them the properties of a magnet.

Either way all magnets have two sides, which we call poles. Just like on the Earth, a magnet has a north pole at one end and a south pole at the other. If you put two magnets together, a north pole will attract a south pole, while a north pole will repel, or push away, another north pole.

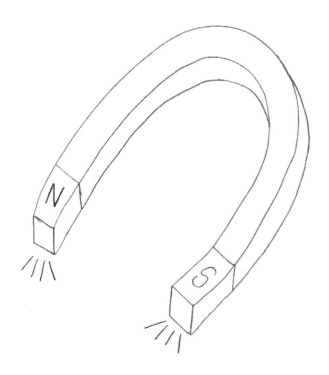

Now it's your turn. I want you to get two bar magnets – those are the long, bar-like ones – and play with them. Try sticking them together and try to get them to repel each other!

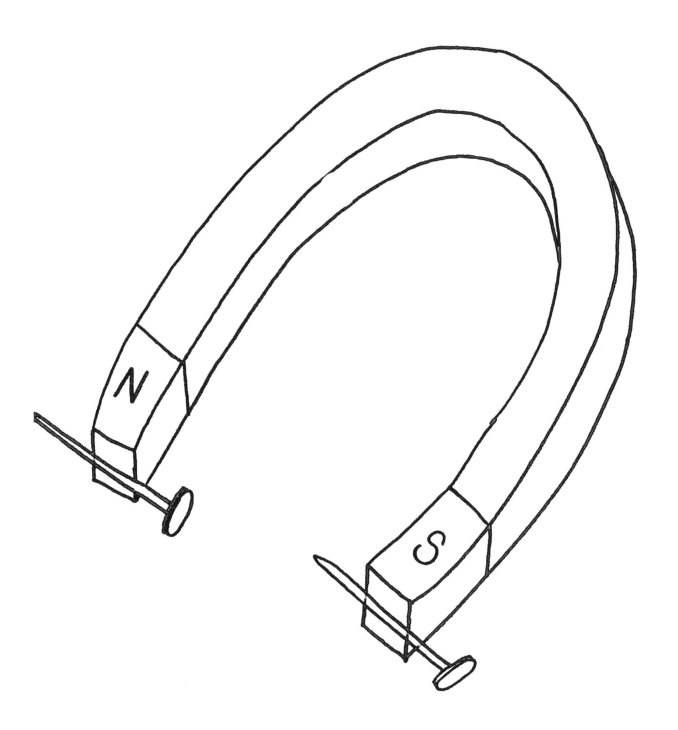

Magnets are attracted to certain kinds of metal.

Magnetic Attraction

Object	Was it attracted to the magnet?	
	Yes	No
	Yes	No
	Yes	No
	Yes	No
	Yes	No
	Yes	No
	Yes	No

Magnetic Art

Unit 8: Energy Lab Manual - Week 4 Magnets

Made in United States
Troutdale, OR
11/30/2023

15169845R00084